Spider on the Moon

A collection of poetry by Paul Vander Loos

A Spider on the Moon

Cover designed by Paul Vander Loos
ISBN: 978-1-64669-182-1

Paul M. Vander Loos
Visit my website at https://wizardsword.wordpress.com

Contents

PROLOGUE

The poems in this booklet were written over several decades and reflect my love of nature, thoughts on life and good-humoured perspectives on people's addiction to mobile phones, moody drivers and going to the dentist among other things.

I have performed some of these poems at various literary events, including the Mackay Festival of Arts, Poets in the Pub, and more recently *Heard Words*. The poetry covers topics like in Brisbane when the then council removed a large Moreton Bay Fig Tree that was a much-loved shady retreat for city office workers; Toowoomba's college cats and sharing a house with other journalism students and insect pests; an encounter with a pup and a one-legged seagull on the beach at Hervey Bay; tributes to late friends and a son who died at birth; and first impressions of the city that I now call home – Mackay.

I hope you will find something among my musings that will relate to you in a meaningful and positive way.

Paul Vander Loos

SPIDER ON THE MOON

Did you know that the moon is like a cup;
It fills from the bottom.
There is a spider on the moon
Moving about
Casting dark shadows across its fingerprint.
I can see its hairs
spreading across the pale white.
It casts its web
And waits.

Nobody knows where the spider went
But the moon is gone too,
Smudged from the sky.
All there is are grey fingers
And the moon's tears
dying to the ground.

The lunatics are wailing
Stumbling in the black night,
Suddenly aware
that they are no longer crazy
except for the maddening hole
in their chests.

Now I am crying,
Shedding tears for a blue moon
And waiting for the spider to return
With the moon in a cocoon.

It never does.

AS THE SUN DIES

As the Sun dies in an ochre blaze
and Brahman cattle in wide fields graze
I drive the Bruce Highway
tired at the end of day,
dreaming of home south of Mackay
where on tropic hills
grasstree spears are shadowed
by sugar mills,
where lazy ships weigh anchor
for the coal to fill the tanker

I hug my A-frame between the stringy barks
and listen to the Australian larks
– the honeyeater, sunbird, kookaburra and black cockatoo
– Rainbow bird, lorikeet and curlew too,
mangroves creak and crackle,
and sandflies whizz
around the fishing tackle
of Cabbage Tree Creek with its winding water green
through the tangle of branches unseen

Yes, home is by the Grasstree shores
where the agile wallaby graze by the score

As the sun dies in an ochre blaze
I turn the bend to end my dreamy daze.

BIRDS FLY

White tufts curl
in the updrafts of the blue,
the flute rises,
transcends,
a cloud whispers by,
leaving droplets
on soft wings
The eye perceives
in tranquil wisdom
(if beaks could smile!)
The beauty, the freedom,
the magic
of flight,
wingtips to eternity;
the bird is commander,
messenger beyond worlds,
vanquisher of gravity,
ruler of the sky.

THE CATS OF THE COLLEGE

Flighty's on the nightshift
at the D.D.I.A.E.
stealing morsels near the refec.
It is a risky trade
No dogs mind you, to worry
but keen-eyed students on the rage,
a hazard for unwary cats
these hunting giants of the paths.

There is *Ginger* and there's *Blackie*
who scavenge through the grass,
to stalk a bird or mouse perhaps,
but mainly food scraps in the bins.

Flighty's two grey kittens
are always peeking in the glass,
curious about that nether world
of D block
sunken in the dirt.

The cats carry on oblivious
of the emotions all around them,
and most students are too busy
to ever notice them.
Two worlds live on, side by side,
each fraught by different dangers,
the cats between their jungle
and the humans in theirs.

GECKOS

I see them here
I see them there
I see those geckos everywhere
They rush up walls
They race down halls
Those geckos with their cheeky calls

They eat up moths, mossies and midges
with a slip of the tongue out behind pictures
They check my mail
through rain, shine or hail
then whisk away with a flick of the tail

I hear their calls both day and night
Cheek—cheep—cheep— cheep—cheep—cheep!
A twirl of the eyes
And they're out of sight
Cheek—cheep—cheep— cheep—cheep—cheep!

GRASS WEBS

How clever you seem
My frightening little comrades;
You with your eight feet
can stitch such intricacy
out of your chemistry.

Yet, for all its concealment,
your careful craftsmanship lay glistening
in the sun's dusty glow ...
Yet, I am amazed that all this
had escaped so long
beneath my feet.

SEASON'S GREETINGS TO A PUP

There's no room at the inn
for a little dog like you,
so don't look at me like that
with those sorrowful eyes
I know the story
but what can I do
for a hungry dog like you?
The gulls have the last scraps,
my plastic bag is empty
and there's no room at home,
besides, it's not my say,
it's not my home.
So why don't you go,
don't hang around, you hear!
and now you have the gall
to bite me on the heel.
I know, but what can I do?
Okay, we'll take a walk
and here's a stick to bite instead,
it seems you're pretty smart,
I wish I could,
I'd teach you well
You'd make a good watch dog,
but you've come at the wrong time
my little friend.

Come along then
just down the beach
to see the people fossick
for crabs and other things;
and so you've had enough,
I've wasted your time,
you've gone to fossick too,
and I go my way.
If only I could
but there's no room at the inn
for a little dog like you.

HOUDINI CROCODILE

He rested at the Gooseponds,
sunning himself with glee
It was Houdini the crocodile
who had come to stay for tea.
Houdini was a cool dude ...
Nothing bothered him,
and when people saw him sunning,
they stopped to see him grin.
He posed for the paparazzi,
dined on fresh duck and fowl,
and when he felt too crowded,
took a dip to escape the howl.
The people of the city
decided he must go;
"There's no room for such a crocodile,
As crocodiles do grow!"
So, the National Parks and Wildlife crew
baited up a trap.
"He'll soon be caught and relocated,
rest assured of that."
But Houdini's tastes were special,
No rancid meat for him;
He ignored the trap and dined on fresh
as fresh is best, by Jim.

Days went by, and then the weeks
as Houdini's fame did spread.
No-one could catch this crocodile
and faces soon turned red.
The people lost their fear of him
as he lounged in the midday sun.
The cameras clicked at this Gooseponds star
and the *Mercury* gave him a run.
But the National Parks and Wildlife crew
were not about to give up chase;
they'd harpoon this wily demon.
It was an open and shut case.

But true to his name, he escaped the barb
And took to the waters cool
where he remains to laugh at the people
In his giant paradise swimming pool.

*The crocodile that the National Parks and Wildlife dubbed
"Crafty" was finally cornered in one section of the Gooseponds
and trapped. He was taken to a croc farm in Far North
Queensland.*

MACKAY NIGHT

Silent, like butterflies, they
The winged black dingoes fly
Away from the fire
That dies in the west
Into the tunnel of night.

Unseen flap of wings
in melaleuca quarrels shrill
Odour of burnt honey drench
the evening's nectar light.

With their burden of dead flies
chlorophyll ants caravan
out of the lost day,
returning to the womb of earth.

Egg-faced plovers cack-cack
in the nocturnal dawn;
Only the rude crickets answer
through the solemn darkness.

THE MARLIN

Weeping fibres,
whistling reels,
turmoil beneath blue waves
Sinking, rising, the boat swells,
wallowing amidst cobalt hills,
and the fish slides away,
a shadow in the wild liquid depths.

The harp string sings
and muscles sweat,
the bow deeply thrust
strains to seek the blue
whose tenuous connection strains so well.

Rapidly, without consent,
reclaimed, the fibre sent,
cobalt waves peel back,
and revealed, the marlin seeks the sky.
With sword that hacks at scolding air,
polished body two toned
flashes amidst white spray.
It wings upon its sail,
dancing urgently upon the fatal fibre
that clings relentlessly.

Man and beast this ritual repeat
till lathered arms and ailing beak,
the fish's struggle lost.
Flesh gaffed and hooked,
it hangs impaled.
Clouded sightless eyes stare tragically,
a thousand pounds of muscle
no longer sleek and free
amongst the bitter sea.

Paul M. Vander Loos

THE MORETON BAY FIG TREE

A stump remains where yesterday there stood
a tree so large, a fig
of Moreton Bay

A century its canopy of green
repaired the aching greys
of buildings, roads and glass windows,
an oasis, fresh and cool
to rest a moment
to breathe the scent of sap and wood,
to drink its shade,
to dream of forests long gone.

A rich man says now it must go,
in its place a building will complete
the aching greys,
the busy street.

Despite the woes of clerk or girl
to protect the grand old lady
from her execution,
to each there steals the hoodless men
at dawn when Christmas was just passed in;
They hacked away her arms
till naked, raped and slashed
only her trunk remains
to greet a sad grey dawn.
Today, Brisbane's grand old fig tree
was gone.

ME AND A ONE-LEGGED SEAGULL

It seemed for one precious moment
we shared souls,
just me and a one-legged seagull
on a tide swept beach,
each balanced precariously
but standing
despite the forces
that pushed at us;
a crazy analogy:
to outsiders;
a comedy of souls
reaching infinity;
merged by limitlessness.
I surveyed his wary yellow eye
then walked away
in silence.

THE PLAGUE OF CROWN STREET

Out of summer's kitchen they came;
came upon tiny black feet,
came upon the burring wing,
came upon the dirt,
the dust, the mouldy fruit,
the scraps,
the leftovers.
They came and they multiplied:
two, four, eight, sixteen,
THIRTY-TWO!
We threw the scraps outside,
cleaned the sludge away,
swept the floor clean,
but still they came.
Midges sprung up around ankles,
flies played cat and mouse
with legs and frantic arms;
cockroaches crept up venetians,
cicadas committed suicide
on lino floors,
moths flew hectic formations,
landing on essays,
honey-coated cups,
or tonight's dinner.
Hairy huntsmen hurried to their deaths,
crushed under heels:
these trespassers of fear.
Yet still they came, this plague,
the insects of Crown Street.

Rainy Days

Grey skies, grey air, grey moods
come hand in hand
in this city in the sky,
where clouds become anchored
on my windscreen
and pour out their sorrows
EVERY-WHERE!
Wet roads, wet clothes,
leaky cars,
smelly cars;
where carpets support pools,
and electrical systems
fail to negotiate
with the eternal damp.
At home, it's better to forget the rain
if you can
and snuggle up to the fireplace,
watching the tickling flames
and listening to the sound of rain
in reverse;

forgetting the soak in your car
while you eat toasted marshmallows
and honey,
watching a movie
or something trivial
and reading *The Bulletin*
at the SAME TIME!
Appetites blossom
which is just as well;
the mould is moving in;
even the window
is green.

THE ANT POEM

I've got a bee in my bonnet
About ants in my pants ...
in my pantry
in my sink
and everywhere you think
a self-despising ant may care to ...
make a link.
They have no care for human beings
and every time I turn around
I see these crowded scenes
of ants making off with breadcrumbs,
making tunnels through my greens,
eating all in sight;
even the foam of the *Koolite*.
They'll eat the sponge
out of my scourers,
the silicone of the fish tank;
they'll find the tiniest trace of food
and march to it in a long rank;
Little orange buggers
Barely a millimetre or two,
they are the biggest bane
and how their numbers grew ...
"Hey, come over to Paul's place,
He's got some food for you!
So, don't miss the banquet
or you'll really spew!"

A Spider on the Moon

Well, I tried to bait the little buggers
Some died but others knew
the bait would just run out one day
and so their numbers grew.
Some entered in the microwave
while it happily zapped away
but all they did was dance
while I just sat and prayed.
The war against the ants,
it seems to go forever,
Perhaps I should move out
so this relationship will sever ...

But I'll never give up
against this minute foe!
I'll fight them in the kitchen
I'll fight them in the dough,
I'll fight them on the window sill,
on every sliding door
I'll drown their scrawny bodies
and squash them on the floor!
I'll smash them with my own bare fists
as they stream into my domain,
I'll not take their tawdry trespass
Not let them make their gain.
I'll rain upon them from above
like a beast insane;
Those dirty little critters
Will hear my voice profane!

Yet ... let me not give you the idea
that I don't care for nature's lot.
Why, every time I sit on my rear
I give it ALL I've got!

THE QUEENSLAND PESTS

They make 'em big in Queensland
They're the biggest pests you'll see
And in numbers you can't count …
They're more than thirty-three!
Why, the flies will make the sky go black,
The fleas will drive a dog insane,
The mossies are so big and fat
they look like a flamin' plane!
One landed in Mackay the other day
The airport staff moved to refuel it …
It was half tanked with Avo
before they knew it!
Me mate said he got a caller …
Fella in a big brown coat.
"Didn't say much … and smelt," he said.
Then he saw that insectine jaw …
It was a cockie – not an in-law.
Then there was that nasty scare
when I woke up in a tree
surrounded by green ants throwing up their bums.
They'd carried me out of bed … you do the sums!

A Spider on the Moon

Yeah, they're mighty big in Queensland
You can't tell the ticks from the cows
The males look like ATVs
and the sheilas like big fat sows.
Now, the midges are small
I'll grant you that
but not in number, not at all ...
A million will bite you around the feet
and you'll end up like you have measles
... red as a beet'
But the worst of all is that invisible mite
that will make you itch like crazy at night.
Just watch it when you walk the bush
The scrub itch will get you
whether you're tough or a wuss.

THERE WAS A WILD DOG

There was a wild dog
It wandered as it pleased
It was free, and limited
only by its senses …
Then one day a man saw it
and captured it …
He put it in a cage
And watched over it.
The man said: "You cannot be free.
You have eaten of my sheep.
You stalk the pasture hillsides
and know every animal as prey.
You did not stop at my fence line;
You did not read my signs
saying 'Trespassers Keep Out!'
Why do you take MY sheep?
Why do you trouble MY land?"

The dog looked out through the bars
and saw that the man had limited him.
He was no longer free
and he said to the man:
"Who are you to put your name on the land?
When tomorrow you will be the soil
You will be the grass the sheep eat
Did YOU make the earth you call your own
or did the earth make you?

Do you limit all things
because you limit yourself?
Is that why you shut out the wind
and close out the sunshine?
Is that why your feet never touch the earth?
The earth you cannot share with your brother!
Do you believe you can capture a rainbow
and keep it in a cage?"

The man regarded the dog and thought
about what it had said.
Then the man said: "You ate my sheep"
and shot the dog dead.

Tranquillity

Tranquillity is a river
speaking soft burbles to the breeze,
a seagull soaring
with only the clouds for company.
Tranquillity is a forest,
green and subdued,
mildness and softness share
tranquillity's grace.

It is a peace
that transcends to the spirit,
so all is balanced and warm,
and loving.
Peace and Love together
create tranquillity.

WHALESONG RECONCILIATION

We thank you Right People
for restoring our kind
We thank you Right People,
you gave sight to the blind,
as we are the whales of the great ocean deep
The Right and the Humpback
returned from our sleep.

We sing our new songs,
songs of communion,
a righting of wrongs,
mammalian union
In the liquid dark waters
you may hear the whales cry
an end to the slaughters,
an end to the lie.

Yes, Orca and Sperm, and grandfather Blue
with Pigmy and Fin Whale, Minke and Sei,
Together we bless you,
breach up to the sky
Right People we hail you
from Perth to Mackay.

And Bryde's Whale and Pilot
all dolphin kind too,
all join with each other
in the oceans of blue,
We swim and we leap,
we dive and we play,
and rejoice for Right People,
Right People today.

We remember those sad days,
Shed tears for the lost
Whale blood filled the bays
We paid the cost,
Right People who cared
fought the cause of our plight
against harpoon they dared
put an end to death's night.

WINTER AT GRASSTREE

The Ibis stalks
with leisured walks,
probing lawns for titbits
in the frosted air
A regent sun stares
out of a spotless veil of blue
and the breezes make cold conversation
through the trees' green hats.
Agile wallabies peek up
from grassy fields,
ears twitching as marble eyes watch;
Their statue forms
hold silent intensity
while I, the man
step along the stony path,
My dog poking his nose
at every new scent,
Unhurried,
caught in the laziness of the day,
His delight to explore
at his master's side.

I smile and call out his name
and like a call to duty
he rejoins me, tail wagging.
The gilded sun slowly falls,
casting long shadows
Birdcall fills the space
between the lonely trees,
Martins make quick circles
low over the field,
An eagle wraps
its wings across the veil;
There are eyes everywhere.

AN AUSTRALIAN LANDSCAPE

What is this sunburnt country
that you love?
Would you love it still
when the kite circles you above?
Would your heart be filled
when the grain withers in the field,
when the sheep bays in the mud?
Does the banker smile and pat you on the back
or does he shake his head, apologise ...
"I'm sorry, it's time to pack ..."
Who put that hole in the sky, anyway!

No ... then what is it that you love?
Six-thirty rising, take the kids to school,
An hour on the freeway breathing smog,
Work in the air-conditioned cool,
Mowing the yard on Sunday,
State of Origin on TV
Living with a Gay,
Chopping down that tree?
No? ...

Then in what dreamtime do you belong?
Has your soul forgot the song?
Have you ever learnt the language
that the gums tell you all day long?
The stones cry out in the wilderness ...
"Awake! Awake!"
and the elders' eyes grow dark
and the young ones stumble in the light
as the Dreamtime loses them
as it has never gained the white.

My friend, open your eyes
and behold the far horizons of your sight.
Never is the Dreamtime lost ...
Only you.

WAITING

Waiting ...
To be born
To breathe, to see, to feel
Waiting ...
To speak, to communicate
To crawl, to stand, to walk
Waiting ...
To be fed, to be nourished
To grow, to develop
Waiting ...
To understand, to learn,
To run, to laugh
Waiting ...
To be loved and to love,
To receive and to give
Waiting ...
For the night and the day,
For the season and the reason
Waiting ...
For struggles to end,
For new beginnings
Waiting ...
For the show to begin,
For the pay and the holiday
Waiting ...
For the pain to end
For the health to return

Waiting ...
At the crossroads,
To decide,
To make a choice
Waiting ...
At the door of opportunity,
In the valley of despair
Waiting ...
Along the road of expectations,
To reach the rainbow of hope
Waiting ...
For a change of heart,
Forgiveness
Waiting ...
For Life to begin
And to end
Waiting ...
To die to self,
To die to earth,
For renewal
Waiting ...
Tick tock, tick tock, tick tock
Don't blame the clock,
Don't blame the sun
That rises and sets
Nor the tide that ebbs and flows,
The seasons, the dry, the rain
Live now ... stop
Waiting ...

Paul M. Vander Loos

THE AUSSIE WAR

I never saw that sandy shore,
I never climbed those hills,
I didn't see the flame and guts
nor heard explosions near

A brown slouch hat I've never worn
nor a khaki uniform,
I've never felt the pain inside
when your mates are blown to bits

I hate the wars and memories,
I'm a peace loving sort of bloke,
yet I feel a tear come to my eye
on that one day of the year

I hear the yarns and see these men
return to days gone by,
for many years I wondered why
but now it's clear to me,
they stood together in conflict,
in mateship beyond compare,
they give to these
their comrades passed
this loyal gift, Lest We Forget –
ANZACs never die.

BLOOD ON THE GUM

There is blood on the gum,
The tall stately gum
It's the blood of a black man
Shot down with a gun
He minded nobody's business
When he climbed that there tree
He was just an Aborigine
Rugged and free.

An eight-year-old boy
Saw the man up a tree
And said to the stockman
Quite innocently ...
"There's an Aborigine in the tree."

The stockman said nothing
When he aimed his rifle high
Shot him like a pig
Waiting to die.
The boy gasped in horror,
Cried all the way home
Sobbed up to his daddy
And let out a moan.
"They shot an Aborigine!
He was up in a tree.
Daddy, why did they do it?
Right in front of me!"

His father sighed long and hard
With a look of resign
Told his son to keep quiet …
"You never mind."
"If we speak out, son.
It's sure to come back
No job for me.
We'll all be done.
It's the way of the land.
No history will tell
About how the blacks died
In a white man's hell."

Seventy years later
Through aged eyes
Tears fall unbidden
When he remembers the lies.
It's there in his memory
As clear as can be.
When there was blood on the gum
And a dead Aborigine.

KALEIDOSCOPE PEOPLE

Have you seen the kaleidoscope people
shouting at you
from behind screens and speakers,
with their guitars and their music,
pale faces
in mists and dream landscapes,
automated motions
shouting at tradition,
screaming at the mirror
society
but it does not shatter;
The oldies squirm then laugh,
ignorance is freedom
at the switch of a knob.
So who listens to the words?

Escape! Escape!
Escape in electronic vibrations,
ecstasy and mania entranced
till the hollow world
calls you back.

Paul M. Vander Loos

THE MIRROR PEOPLE

The bird in the cage
whistles in a fantasy
to its image in a mirror,
the only company
except for the people
who call him 'Pete'
and whistle and smile at him
then walk away

But no less caged are we
than Pete,
caged by our wants
in capsules we amble,
acting out charades
to self images,
lost in false reality.
Nobody knows who we are
because they don't know their selves,
only glass images.

Sweet Nothings

From Kookaburra's laugh
To flying fox complaint
Each day is filled
With sweet nothings.
It's too early
It's too cold
I'm too young
I'm too old,
The toast is burnt
There's no bread
I feel sick
I'm almost dead,
The weekend was too short
The week is too long
I've got too much to do
My life is all wrong,
The dog barks too much
The cats fight all night
I didn't get enough sleep
Will we ever get it right?
It's too late
It's too hot
It's too wet
It's too dry,
There's pests in the crop
The government's crook
Petrol prices are up
The bank has gone bust

The boss is a woman!
The boss is a man!
Too much work
For too little pay
Can't afford to keep the kids
Too few hours in the day,
The air and water's polluted
The country is rooted
All the soil's gone to sea,
No more trees
Too much poison
Armageddon is here
Too much apathy
But who cares,
It's all sweet nothings
To our ears!

TEMPORARY POEMS

I'm chasing shadows
in my mind
while my heart runs
amongst the clouds,
I write my temporary poems
about temporary people
wanting to love
forever.
In the fleeting dreams
the future blinks past,
shining a tiny ray of hope
Goodness comes
to those who wait.

PEOPLE

We call ourselves aware
We call ourselves wise
We call others fools
We choose our own lies
To believe
That white is better
That black is worse
That yellow is sickly
That others are a curse

Day follows night
As we evolve in the Light
Of the one who dared the truth
To give back our sight

He said we are equal,
All children of God
That Heaven's the sequel
For this mighty mob.

SOME DAYS I'M ... BEACHES

Chorus: Some days I'm ... Beaches
Some days I'm ... Rock
Some days I'm ... Mountain
And some days I'm ... not.

Every day the sun comes up
and I fill my cup,
Life is getting up each day
so from this cup I sup.

With each day I learn some more
I forget the hurts and pain,
I pray to my God above,
my shelter in the rain.

The years drift past
like misty mornings in the gloaming,
I drink from my cup of life,
keep up my endless roaming.

Then at the day's end sunset
I take my last few sips,
I'll leave this life in peace
with wisdom on my lips

THE CHILD

In the ocean I saw her,
A child in trouble
Waving for help
Waving at me on the beach
In a shroud of mist, mourning
But I could do nothing
I had no legs
No voice to cry out
No means to rescue her.

Would she endure
Until she washed up on my stone
For I was the rock.

TO ANDRE – 7/12/97

I sit on the edge of the abyss
where I cast my 'whys' like petals
into the hole that cannot be filled
nor can I call back
what is lost in the mist below

The abyss is my heart
in which our baby dwells,
but not his presence swells,
nor his warm breath felt

Why is our baby in the ground?
all still, not making a sound,
No cry but ours pours forth
as they 'whys' fall.

No answer flies up from darkness,
only our forest of 'whys' rain down,
even God is silent, unyielding
and we sit at the abyss of our hearts.

WHEN THE RAINBOWS LEAVE YOUR EYES

When the rainbows leave your eyes
They'll fall in teardrops from the skies
The sun will disappear from view
The earth will cloak itself in dew
Grey clouds will gather, heaving dark
Raindrops bring splashes in the park
Where daffodils glimmer in nodding yellows
Reflections murmur across the shallows
Frogs appear in their green tights
Blinking black pearl eyes
Against the nights

A dog's silhouette in the shadows stalks
Sniffing where his master walks
With shining eye he lifts his head
And you awake from in your bed

With the rainbow tears you shed
You listen to the water
Dripping from the eaves
And plopping softly over leaves
Filling pools at your door

You remember when you were Four

When the rainbows leave your eyes
Your life will fill with sighs.

TRUTH IS LIKE ...

Truth is like ...
Like one of those surprise gifts
That sets up false expectations
In minds that equate size
And the quality of the gift.
They peel away at the wrapping
Only to discover another beneath;
The gift diminishing
With each layer
Until despairing,
Disappointed,
The recipient
Suspects
Some trinket ...
Some clothed subterfuge,
A scam
Falsehood
Deception
Deceit ...
But as the final layer peels back
Truth is revealed at its core;
Lustre fine like gemstone
A priceless reward.
And really, size had nothing
To do with it
At all.

LOVE IS LIKE ...

Love is like ...
Like the many-layered Truth;
It's unexpected
Never the image
Like a book's cover.
Not the impassioned expression
Of some frozen visage
Caught in conflict
While the hero fights some obstacle
To be by another's side.
That's romance;
And Love is larger than desire,
Larger than a moment of lust,
Larger than the image;
Only you still
Don't see it
Because dimensions
Are immaterial;
It's something quite unexpected,
But without it
The wheels will
Fall off,
The cogs will stop,
Life will die
Forever
And Hell begin.
And really,
The image has nothing
To do with it
At all.

LIFE IS LIKE ...

Life is like ...
Like a game with no rules,
Just bundled up packages masquerading
As things, like Love and Truth,
Only our expectations
Are always the measure
Of how well we do;
How much we realise
That the stage
Is constructed
Of holograms
And what our senses
Tell us
Isn't real at all.
We must find the mirrors,
Switch off the laser imaging
And look at ourselves,
Knowing
The people we are shouting at
Are clothed clones
Of ourselves.
And that really
The packages
Have absolutely nothing
To do with it
At all.

WHERE IS GOD?

Some people say that
God is in heaven
But I just saw him
Only a moment ago.
I was walking with my dog
When there he was
In the golden sunlight;
Through the rain-fresh leaves
She whispered in the wind
And moved through the trees.
I saw him in the rainbow,
I saw her flying
In the eagle
And in the waves
Washing to the shore;
I saw his shadow in the clouds
And the scent of her
In the salt air;
I felt him in the sand
Beneath my feet;
I heard her laughing
Her kookaburra laugh;

I felt his life
Coursing through my blood;
I touched her eucalyptus smoothness,
I breathed his air.

Did you say God is in heaven?
Then maybe heaven
Is right
Here.

Paul M. Vander Loos

Jams and Preserves

Remember the corner store
Glass shelves under the counter
Lollies galore
Two or three for a cent
And more.
All around there are wondrous things
Like a mini-market
And on one shelf – a sign
"Jams and Preserves".

Remember the smiles
Of store staff,
The rotund woman
With her small talk;
The man who knows you by name
Handing you a free lolly
And a pat on the head.
"See you tomorrow," he says,
And the labels on the jars and cans
"Jams and Preserves".

Those were carefree days,
Days of pushbikes,
School bus runs,
Ports slung over backs,
Secret conversations
And curdling mysteries
Around every corner,
And warm sandwiches
With cheese or ham
Or sweet spreads
"Jams and Preserves".
Day follows day
Year chases year
Soon youth is gone
And times change,
Corner stores are rare,
Their shelves dusty, forgotten,
Sheltering old trinkets
With faded print
And long-gone use-by dates;
Smiles are rare,
Hypermarkets corral
Herds of blank faces;
Only the sign remains
– "Jams and Preserves".

Paul M. Vander Loos

THE CUP

Every person in Australia
is a punter for a day
when the Melbourne Cup is racing
in November of each year

All business stops in homes and shops
in every state and town
as the greatest horse race of the year
prepares for another run

The starters fidget behind the gates,
the bookies close the bets,
a nation sits and bites its lips
as the gates are open swung

Astride the leap, a mass of horse meat
lunging at the gallop,
ripping turf and tossing dirt
onto the field the run

The caller sings his racing tune
of lads and boys and toys,
the horses vie and the jockeys fly
floating over rolling rumps

Then comes the turn, the crowd is roaring,
the caller sings an urgent beat,
the greys and browns are merging
as they come into the stretch

The calls and cries and flying dirt
all reach into crescendo
as the sweating beasts all compete
in this last great dash for fame

A Spider on the Moon

The leaders strain and inch and wane,
the post is lengths away,
the crowd is roaring, the singer calling,
the Cup is in the sway

The winner takes the post,
the places in behind,
the Cup has been decided,
it's another race, another year

The losers count their losses,
the winners grin and dance away
and they all talk about the favourites
that didn't make the day

The Cup has passed another year,
the nation goes about its business,
until the next November day
when the ritual is repeated.

A Tribute to John Smith

A brush upon his lips
John pens a world of colour.
Limbs fail to obey;
flailing, stammering hands
barely control his chair.
John rides out the pain
to complete the picture;
his mouth like deft fingers
drawing paint in delicate lines,
lovingly caressing the canvas.
Multi-hued parrots take flight;
coral fishes dash across reef landscapes,
Life in all its beauty emerges vibrant.
The man who conquered so much
no longer surveys the canvas,
yet his beautiful children
continue to delight
the eye.

Rest now in Jesus' arms
John Smith.

To Keith Willey

There will be a ripple
On your lake the day
When you decide to leave ...
The whispering breeze will wait to say
Goodbye with a wave of the trees.

The Rock will scratch the Springs' blue sky
A bloodied ochre hue,
And the drovers' ghosts
Will howl through the dingo,
Howl til' the kangaroo ...
Til' the kangaroo
Looks up.

Paul M. Vander Loos

TO MARTIAL ARTISTS

Motion swings
in curves the body dances
like some ballet;
yet beyond
the hand is alive
and the foot lifts high:
CONTACT!
The martial artist strikes
then swings and curves
to elude the other's blow,
in smooth motions,
each curve upon curve,
slicing through the air,
each movement controlled
but swift like lightning,
so each blow counts,
blows that once could main a mighty foe
to leave the pack
crawling in the dust,
senseless

The martial artist is alert,
his perception is control,
only the mind perceives
to conquer:
matter is eliminated by mind,
crystallised
in this paradox —
tranquility.

MOBILE MADNESS

You find them on street corners
Stuck to someone's ear
And in busy offices
With people on their rear,
Like buzzing black cicadas
They call out in refrain
Those annoying little mobiles
That driver us all insane.

They're found in toilet cubicles
Where privacy is no more
And invade our sacred places
And on every nation's shore;
Even the church and library
Echo to their sound
Those annoying little mobiles
Upwardly mobile, outward bound.

In our dining venues
Now smokers change their tone
Instead of lighting Winfields
They switch on their mobile phone;
It's enough to drive you crazy
This digital invasion
Those annoying little mobiles
Sing at every occasion.

I can hear them everywhere
With their many varied songs
And people chatting happily
Going hammer and tongs.
They wear them boldly on their hips
In smart leather cases
Those endearing little mobiles
That every person chases.

Telstra, Optus and Vodaphone
Compete for your attention,
They are a status symbol
With numbers too long to mention.
You can pay right through the nose
Or buy a pre-paid model
Those wonderful little mobiles
That we moddle-coddle.

ROAD RAGER

There is no time to stop and chat
I have to get to work
I'm in a flaming hurry
And I'm about to go berserk
The traffic's banked up to the bridge
There is no room to move
So come on you in the beat-up van
Get ya bum in gear, now man!

Oh, for heaven's sakes
What's wrong with you?
Catch up to the other cars!
You had a thousand chances
I'll make you see some stars!

BARP! BARP! BARP!
AHAH! A chance to pass!
Take that you bloomin' idiot!
Put that up your (bleep)!

Now, what's that coming up ahead
She didn't use her blinker!
SCREECH! SCREECH!
Friggle! Frazzle! Growl! Gruzzle!
You stupid little stinker!

I've had enough of idiots
And time is running out
I'll ignore this light that's just turned red
And drive on through, no doubt

... BEEBLE! BEEBLE!
Oh, what damn rotten luck!
Hello officer – I'm sorry sir
It's just that I was stuck
I'm in a kinda hurry
... well yes, the fine's two hundred bucks?

SUNDAY DRIVER

Hello, fellow motorists
I'm pleased to meet you all
I'm your friendly Sunday driver
Who'll drive you up the wall

Why, to me motoring's a pleasure
When I embark upon the road
I savour every moment
With my precious people load

There are many views and scenes
As we tour along our way
Let us take it as tour leisure
We have all this fine long day.

The road is such a friendly place
Every motorist gives a toot
Then they show me one long finger
And scream: "Why don't you walk, you silly coot!"

I'm the man who wears the hat
With a queue behind, a mile long
As I cruise at 40 kay
Whistling a happy song.

In my six-cylinder Mercedes
My motor just on cool
I turn my indicator on
As I veer towards the school.

Oops, I forgot to look to my right
But that nice lady saves the day
Her car has such good brakes
So, I continue on my way.

Now we end our journey
Turn left into my drive
Everyone is safe and sound
And I am still alive.

WHY

I know it is inevitable
In every child's days
That the question must be posed
That no-one can erase

The question seems quite simple
But it's worrying as a pimple
It slips by in one quick syllable
Yet the impression is indelible

No greater question can be asked
And no answer can be found
For no sooner do you answer
Then another level comes around.
And it is that same dogged question
That smacks you in the face,
Harder than 'green eggs and ham'
Can YOU hack the pace?

Oh why do we give them this power?
Why, oh why, oh why?
I am caught in this infinity
And I fear that I must lie.

Why?
There is no reply
Yet they will not give up
They will not accept a sigh.
I can only shrug or pass the buck,
"Go and ask your mother."
But soon the four-year-old returns
To query with another!

Pregnant

I don't like your breath, my darling
I don't like my breath too
I feel nauseous most of the day
Like I'm about to spew

I'm sleepy in the morning
And sleepy all the day
I'm sleepy in the evening
Oh darling, what can I say

Please close the door behind you
I don't like the smell of food
You see all of that fine cooking
Makes me sick, sorry I'm rude

It's all your fault, my darling
You made me feel this way
Now don't disturb my baby
Wherein my womb it lay

So, no more sex, my darling
At least until I'm due
Well, just this once I tell you
But no more till it's due.

AN EXTRACT IN MEMORIUM

Alas, poor molar
I knew him well,
we had dined together
and wined together
for many years
He fought valiantly
through Mars bars,
peanuts,
cakes, biscuits, ice-cream
and a host of food encrustations
He warned me that he didn't like the cold:
that was a mutual hate.
It brought me much pain
to see the old fellow go;
We tried to save him.
"Dentists are not God,"
said the executioner,
then pulled him out,
leaving me swimming in my blood.

I'll mourn his passing
for that respectful time
and assure his mates
remain to dine.